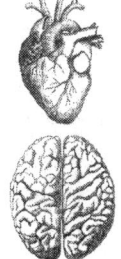

OUR BODIES & OTHER FINE MACHINES
Natalie Wee

WORDS DANCE PUBLISHING
WordsDance.com

1st Edition
ISBN-13: 978-0-9979404-3-5
ISBN-10: 0997940433

Cover design & interior layout by Amanda Oaks & Natalie Wee
Cover photograph by Natalie Wee

Type set in Roadgeek 2005 Series 1B & Bergamo

Words Dance Publishing
WordsDance.com

OUR BODIES & OTHER FINE MACHINES
Natalie Wee

I.

The most beautiful part of your body
is where it's headed. & remember,
loneliness is still time spent
with the world.

Ocean Vuong, *"Someday I'll Love Ocean Vuong"*

OUR BODIES & OTHER FINE MACHINES

I.

MIRROR

Sometimes, she told me, *liking someone*
is just a way to pass the time.

Each illicit word a loose tooth slipping
from the open mouth of our class flirt—

the kindest name fourteen-year-olds pinned
to a girl infamous through every grade

for tucking teachers' names under her tongue
as if forbidden candy in place of hunger.

See, we hadn't understood yet where the
empty comes from even though we had

been told girls were always wanting to be
filled. How, across the vast foyer that held only

waiting, sunlight launched silver curveballs
off the sleek roof of every car rounding

the smooth driveway & yet never quite
caught our shadows. Her arm, bright with

sweat, near enough to radiate dangerous heat.
I thought she meant pretending the way

every bright carriage becomes a cool hand
in an afternoon buzzing with searching bodies

so I breathed *I understand* into the space
separating any two mouths. But I didn't

know, then, how waiting turns the waking
hours into one long stretch for tomorrow

until the makeshift relief of fiction turns
into the tenuous thing itself. Once,

beyond outflung classroom doors, I saw
her touching herself under battered desks

with a blacksmith's hands. The shape of
loneliness splintering a body into pathways

out of fear. The precarious attempt to know
wholeness not as sensation but indescribable

matter. Her fingers moving fast & brutal
as if mapping blue edges of the unseen sky.

This is what it means to really want
something. Her open mouth an iris ringed

with desperation deeper than shame. *You'll*
forsake everything if only to be real—

LETTERS FROM PERSEPHONE
after Tara Mae Mulroy

      Waited so long

for fruit mama

      I found it   ripe

between antlered thighs

      in the fields my

skull was a crown

      set on foundations

of desire   he

      was my first

act of godhood

              body

      resurrected from un

-speakable places to

      be mine

      Mama I did

not forget   sweat

      from my palms

washed

      the animal of

him marble

      the way you

taught me

      to cradle wounded

things

      cleaned those

bones with my own

                    good mouth
                                his
fingers
        wingspan
                my jaw open

this
is how
you break the earth
for desire

        Beneath dirt
my skin blooms
        nightshade   oh
                    mama we
are luminary   doves
        where nothing
                        flies his
hair river
        reeds full
moon every night
                he coaxes
                        spring

        from inside me

JESUS TAKES ME TO BED

You a forest & god with eyes of a wild thing—
                                    her body a shape beyond

                        pronounceability. Unraveling scripture
            as pelt on tongue: yours / hers. Fingers
                    unearthing a doorway to paradise.

Dew down the throat: flesh fissured for starlight. The
                        swallow: the only communion that delivered
            its promise. Church says, god is good. But she is best

in your mouth. Lucifer is in hell because she loved her
                    in a way that was not understood. Nightly
        you practice resurrection by fire,

                        rechristening in the river you swim through
                to find something worth redeeming.
        Your head bowed, nursing the secret to un-

    death at her breast. God does not live
                    in church. She made you her kingdom. Of course
she lives in you.

THE THEORY OF MAGIC

Like any other witch I was born from desire
& all true witches know to be desired

is to destroy. Mine was not a magic
of large curses but small misfortunes.

No death / illness / calamity. Only a mouth
full of knives where longing expects raw

meat. Hands that turn river stones when
asked for water. Thighs smooth as

thistle & strangling fig: my fruit sweet
as homespun confections & tender

as teeth. Enough to break a jaw on.
Maybe even a heart. I know the ways

of my sisters. Some melt stars for crowns.
Some swallow wicked creatures & become

them. I am steel trap crowned with
a magpie's glint: not a girl to be saved but

a girl to be saved from. I wear elixir /
ecstasy / escape as god wears proof

of cruelty like power. What can a death be
but fierce, in spite of who loves it—or

perhaps because it is loved? What can
I be but unaccountable, when they knew

& still wanted ruination?

EITHER/OR/OTHER

Tell me where to go.
Years ago silver screens radiated

car swerves & sickbed blues & now
stray bullets splinter Technicolor lovers

into ghosts of another century—
but any girl who touches another with

intent still wears the color that hurt
girls like me. I practice unraveling

the secret of being queer/brown/woman
separately so maybe I can be happier

with two-thirds of a full life. A crowd
at Pride Toronto smites Black Lives Matter

while I watch fans of *The 100* bury any proof
that the furious kiss of two sallow women

only glowed when set against a backdrop
of dark bodies.

What is it like to be made a person
instead of a stranger's dim shadow?

What does it mean to have a mirror
if not to see your self whole—

no matter the scars, the inconvenience of being
alive to interrupt someone else's pleasure

instead of staying dead?
The wait is heavy with years: to be seen,

then seen & not killed. Yet
under heavy snow in a barren field

where nothing grows, my bones are heavy
                                    with the weight

of never having been seen at all.

(SUICIDE LETTER IN) PARTS, 2010

Childhood furnished by bruises
& simple rules:
every day you trip.
Every day
sharp corners want a kiss.

You gave it to them.
You chose.
Measuring the distance
between moving body
& unstoppable force—
sea, traffic, knife—

shredding fingers
between grimy incisors
to prove you can own pain
back:
you chose that, too.

To prove you held something
living in your animal mouth.
To prove something wanted
to be held.
By you.

What would you look like,
if you weren't cut
with a knife doused in loss?
Would you know
yourself if not for

two decades of gravestones
without bodies?
If you stopped fantasizing about
strangers who looked at you

long enough to prove you could
be seen?

Girl
                    even loneliness leaves
            like a ghost tired of haunting
                    someplace no one visits.

                            The derelict cinema
                where you tried to grow love
            in a flimsy shoe box,

                            the same movie playing
                for eight years.

    How every beautiful girl
                vanishes in that gap,

                how silence knifes deeper
                    the longer it keeps—

                    your tongue an empty gun.
        To be so lonely
                    you told yourself you liked to be this way

                & almost believed
                            it was true.

                Name yourself
        something that stays
                    no matter the wound.

                        What's synonymous
        for a state of being when
                    your own body doesn't want
                to be yours?

ENOUGH TO LEAVE

Someone always loves more. We blame this
on fate / facetious coin tosses if moving objects

controlled their orbit. Like which side of toast
kisses carpet, only gravity knows the secret of

endings. Of course I liked the sweet buzz
of you folding over my apple orchard. The

thrum of small, winged planes, nestled amongst
fruit wet with the want of picking. Your earth-

bound hands rivering a new road away from
the skyline where I was born. Meanwhile

my heart waits its season. Shrinks at the steady
pace of amber leaves shedding fall. In winter

the desperate burn their childhood homes when
the last haggard tree is gone. Do you understand?

I was lightning long before you were bird. We
were never meant to alight the same branch &

nest among that which you loved. You offer
sweetness that needs a mouth to melt in when

I do not eat. It will turn sour dough, fester
the longer it goes untouched until it undresses

to a single pitted stone, coarser than the peach it
could have become, swelling fit to choke.

I offer heat that requires sacrifice when there
is only body left to burn. You want to be held

as if a dream in sleep, but I will hold you so long
there will be nothing left. I know the weight of

a beautiful thing ending in my hands, that a thing
of water cannot keep a fever without vanishing.

Look out at the cloudless drought, every bare
trunk hewn grey ash. There is no merciful ending

except the one we carve here.

BLUE MOON

The first kiss feels so much like flying

you can hardly bear it: ribs opening

to rain, feet two fleeting steps from

the last memory of your father's voice.

He is in the next room, hands powderkeg again.

Every notch of your curved spine knows

                        the precise pin & lift
of detonation

& mind still an old gun with petty crimes

carved in. Namely: unlawful escapes.

But then a beautiful mouth blooming.

The un-bruising of a throat made

poppy. The trajectory of every coin

to wishing well reversed: levitation.

Isn't it good, god, to hold a miracle

between your teeth & bite as hard

as your kindness allows—

the choice of something living & raw

between your animal molars, tasting blood

that isn't your own. Your father

is in the next room of another house.

There is no house. There is no room

here. You are continent away from

what foregone dirt that knew only knee.

Unclutch that belly. There is

no wound. Only the ache of realizing

your heart belongs to you.

PRACTICE MAKES PERFECT

for Marie Kakhniashvili

I miss you like a cloud passes right
through skin.
Like everything I've lost,

I make deals with fate
& ask for you back.
Your name tucked under
my tongue, an unraveling

string that pulls
& pulls.

There is no exit
from your language
when it has reached its way
into the recesses of

my chest like a fist, pushed
at the ceiling of diaphragm
like phantom stillbirth.

How loss not an event,
but a process of living past
absence. Mourning is, after all,

a natural state of being.
Vertigo taught our limbs this,
which is why fall comes
so much easier than climb.

How that collapse can stretch into
a shape so solid you'll
spend your whole life on your knees through fire
if only for a drink of water.

I know every river has an end.
You loved me & then you left.

You loved me & then you didn't.

I water myself nightly,
but by dawn I'm parched again.
I know a lot about leaving,
but it never gets easier.

ON AVERAGE, HUMAN BEINGS SURVIVE 7 DAYS ON WATER ALONE

Someone once said the average friendship
lasts seven years. I've watched this number

whittle down to the fingers of a hand caught
in the wave of goodbye. Traded codewords

to belonging as a fallen hiker clutches rope.
If un-loneliness is miracle that requires more

than one body, let me confess I am lonely
like a disaster movie survivor stranded

between perpetual cold shoulder & fiery tongue.
What I know beyond my own heartbeat

is waiting for tidal waves through revolving
doors, moving with the ebb & swell as

the water swallows every self I've been
before now. As if I've always been waiting.

When the worst has already happened, any
smoke turns into a familiar exit sign.

An old fear turns mouth into apology into
vanishing, if only because I've lived through

leaving but not being left behind. & yet I
remember building a path, the weight of

tomorrow the shape of a life. Take me with you
& I will brave dark woods for your kindling

splinter bone for your next meal & build
fires with my body before the last season's

first snowfall. None of this is to say I am good,
too long alone to have been touched by

something real. I am sorry if my fingers tremble.
I promise they can hold anything that knows

staying. Open them & see for yourself
each history of fidelity, so much like

traversing an uninhabited childhood
home & discovering a tattered box once

big enough to contain the whole world.

CLOSE ENCOUNTERS
for Braidon Schaufert

We swap ghost stories,
the future being one of them.
Amidst swerving mountain darkness
the city lights fell away like fields of grain
bent under wind. We crossed
the border between realms & in between
I grasped the shadow of future loneliness.
The way the moon needs night
to hold the pupil illuminated
but also drowns in it.
Phantoms are visible only under
certain conditions. All supernatural
enthusiasts know this. Do not acknowledge
that which is beyond your dominion.
& so I turned. The unsayable hung
in our mouths like melting
freeway snow. Overhead
neon signs swallowed our bodies
& vanished after. Your skin washed
bloodless as we watched streetlights
for answering stars.
The distance between two bodies
measured in sky:
road bellies opened & we held
our own shut.
Alone & afraid are mostly
the same thing. We were both.
We were both here. Your face shone
the first safe beacon I had ever seen.
I held on to that light
as a moth that knows night is coming
chooses to burn.

THINGS TO WATCH OUT FOR

We have always known how to be monsters.
We have play-acted at killing since

we tore into the world. Knife as hand
reaching for candy. Masked or unmasked.

It is not the given but the giving
that we want. The thrill of invitation.

To bury our hands in someone else
& be thanked for what grows. Even

if that is fire. Even if someone beautiful
burns. Mouth an organic weapon holding

the heart at fissure point. The body a room
full of ghosts we never hold quietly

enough. Instinct says: pursue all things
bright & impossible. Pets breakneck

themselves for neon. We build telescopes,
crush lonely into light. We practice all

our lives. We keep love like the horizon
catches a falling star. Like taking a moment

by its throat hides the bruising. How
all that is unforgivable dissolves as long

as something survived our holding. How
the larger fear will win out like a blade

outshines tooth: what does it mean to be
afraid if not alone. What does it mean to be

alone if not real. We say something is real
when it terrifies us. We terrify ourselves.

II.

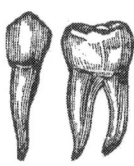

LEAST OF ALL

The space between my head
& hand is the size of peace
of mind. Last week, I counted forty-two
burgeoning dandelions

as they reached for wingtipped
blue. People call them weeds.
All they know of passing time is avoiding
the crush, wearing

the color of happiness into a battle
-field where being pretty means
staying un-buried.
Circling sunbursts for treasure, all dogs

track new shadows through
the underbrush, forever
measuring distance between head
& tail. How long can they walk

the same path? Long enough
that humans built machines to count
steps, feet planted in shapes of retroactive guilt,
silver eyes spun to the ceiling

every raw seed worships because
we will always choose a window over
the mirror someone's looking out of,
asking to stay when

we've swallowed every
other damaged thing—*we can travel
without moving,* that mouth says,
this planet does it

every day—two lips opening
like petals in a blaze. How

I will always end up un
-earthing myself each time
I kneel into a dream where I
am good & loved. I am

good. I am loved. My hands have made
some good mistakes. They can always

make better ones.

THAT KIND OF GOOD
for Caitlyn Siehl

Some people have a softness
that draws water from the earth

Call it dream. Call it flight.
The opening & closing of

your eyelids, like sparrow wings
beckoning the trees.

The music of your bones,
startling spring from the earth,

the dazzle of your smile
drawing honey from the bees.

You are kinder than the cruelest thing
that's ever been done to you.

You are softer than the tender meat
you were bruised into becoming.

You are so good, bad people would
break every hard word over their knees

to keep you from falling on yours.

You are so good, lazy people would
line up to be the coffee-mug at your mouth

if it meant another hour of ease.

The religious talk about the second coming
& you talk your shadow into starlight.

If you asked the clouds for shade
the sky would split itself like apple.

If you asked me to cut out my heart
I would do it with my own knife.

SUBTERRANEAN

Nightly we turn in sleep. Call it
the body's echo of the earth.
A return to the river where sun & moon
wink out of the same face.

We dive, pinioned between knowing
& not. The dreamy film rushing
through fingers as wind skims
turret-trees outside the city.

There, between two palms: a new bird
on the cusp of flight. That animal flutter
unstirring grit & reprimand into softer shadows.
Tongue unspooling the alphabet of distress
signals past. Sheets tracing

the furrows where careless incisors thought
to carve out a desolate yearning.
In the darkness: your underbelly
fluorescent, target-marked by an open window.

Across your sloping ribs,
where no cold has ever been: the sky's glow softening

worn bones to light.

STING

I love you like a bitten tongue:
        fleshy limb incised to keep secret

from speech. Restless copper sting
        drawn forth on rows of solitary

silver hooks. Mouth gorged on desire
        until the jaw splinters like ripe fruit

by falling. The instant between crunch
        & pain is swollen with the pause

of disbelief. Like our first meeting,
        when you told me you've only

been held by boys with a full set
        of teeth & yet never made themselves

tender wound. How can
        any false lover claim to have

given everything when they
        pronounce your name without

lightning, when your questions
        incite brisk answers instead of

a cotton rasp over the skin's
        shiver like undressing in reverse—

who else steeped your name in
        mouthfuls of blood, nursed it as one

must an ancient god that speaks
        only in cuts? To offer one's body in

the gradient of claiming is to
        know it will not stay whole. Here

are my arms, my legs & torso
        leading to the flinty skull cradling

the only muscle able to turn desire
        into speech into sacrifice. Here is

your cup, here is the sweet wine I held
        in my throat for two years without

letting go bad. Come, drink before
        I am dry. Drink before I forget

how long I have slept with knives
        inside my mouth.

SILVERFIN

It should've been one year this December,
but instead it's just my birthday. My

new dress wears my birth colour.
I'm sorry for leaving home. What

flounders know of days is taking
after coral. What I know of survival

is being a shadow. This language
still necessity my blood hasn't

outlived. Science contemplates seahorses
in love, tethered by the promise ring

of prehensile tails—a merciful island
the size of *despite*. How was I to know

that I wouldn't get to choose
the red country I grew out of?

That my family would be split
rafts in messy tidepools, each

meandering down a different antler
in a wishbone river we once knew

like a pondskater's debut waltz. If
we should ever meet again, whether

by migratory fortitude or the precise
accident of swollen moon calling shore,

I want them to know I was always
worse at biology than I laid claim to

otherwise. Wasted all this sea air holding
salt in my mouth. I thought to dive through

the dark cave I was born in—
only to propel myself into another.

Still tropical fish in distant water scored
through with bones. Once I imagined

my country saying *I am sorry for not*
being big enough for you to grow out

of sooner. You, always leaping upstream,
hook-teethed and flashing silver, a

reminder that the most beautiful
things will kill us. I hope the ocean

loves you so much you feel free in its
arms. Now I imagine the triumphant

tide, vengeful swallow awaiting
a citizen of searching. Mother

-land, I hope you don't forgive me.
I know I still haven't.

STATISTICALLY SPEAKING, WE ARE PROBABLY HAPPY ELSEWHERE

after Gaby Dunn

Where salt knows us like backhand
you are band-aid to my bruise. Transparent

as all lies are. Under your body
blood vessels rise like a city's starbursts

in violet. In an art fair our photographs
would hang over strangers like the sun

in orbit. The glow of our faces
backwashing the sky into sepia:

a burning so fantastic ruin looks
like the best story we can tell ourselves.

When night is the size of astonishment
I am the only moon you wish on. The

whole sky systoles of Christmas lights,
each flicker between now & someday

marking distance in light years.
There is nothing else you call miracle.

Around my neck I wear that given name
the way a rocket wears its collision—

the kiss of our meeting a cataclysm
snapping a newborn planet into life.

When the earth sets its scorching into
dull roar of parch we are the last trees

to know forgetting. Before the earth gives
over to sleepshudder they whittle us for

a ramshackle cottage. Forfeit memory
made real. During the holidays, tourists

                    come inside us to make love. We make
                    a temple for desire out of floorboards &

the secret of forever. Which is staying.
& when fire discovers the hiding-place

                              of what ends after us & smoke rings
                              blanket us a warm goodnight—

we turn inside ourselves like marrow
inside moon bone. Every sigh escapes

                         like so much space in every tomorrow
                         when you give me togetherness &

my hands are ready to hold.

HOW TO SAVE YOUR OWN LIFE

        put down that gravestone
    you've been carrying. bury
the people who leave.
             why bear the dead
       when slivered ghosts are everywhere?

stop holding your heart out
    to strangers like grocery samplers,
         hoping they'll covet the tired sun
under all that lonely.
        people who love lonely people
    are always trying to forget.

        you know this because
you are one of them.
         & that's okay.
        exhale what did not serve you
    as firefighter pulls bodies
from the wreckage.
         you are the wreckage,
     you are the fire &
           you are also holding an axe

    which is all to say
        that you are trying to save yourself
from yourself.

    depression is only
           an overstaying visitor who forgets
   who actually owns this body:
        feet that guttered the earth
     to find a place for staying

& a mouth
    that swallowed all poisons
       to earn immunity by the tongue.

it is whole without
            anyone else in it. in your hand
the knife-edge glinting:
            there is
no monster here,
            only the shape of a falling star
where your heart should be.

            northbound & reaching, a
hero telling her story. it starts
            like this: once upon a time,
you rode the dragon

            & saved your own life.

#THINSPO

Every night I practice the taxidermy
of size two skinsuits, recreate the feat

of shrinking yellow women. I Benjamin
Button a mouth that fills itself with empty,

clam up trapdoor to throat that has
forsaken swallow. A hungry audience

watches the tufted clouds emerge:
pale cotton rabbiting from one

damp tunnel to the next. The real
mystery: belly or porcelain?

This body holds me like some great
invisible thing keeps anchorites

captive. There is no leaving this coffin
I made myself. Vanishing courts

with gifts of acid gums toothbrush
heaving so much loss I run out

of room. This cruel & unfaithful
lover—all day it visits girls like me

& kisses them so hard they mistake
worth for waif & learn worship

at altars of absence. I learned
punishment is power the way

my sister cuts herself in half for
the cool kiss of a knife's edge.

But look at the shackles with teeth
that do not bite. Look at the secret

compartment the size of survival,
its intelligent hinges & clever throat

holding me like a creature afraid to die
alone. Look at how much space

escapes its hold, how its shadow lengthens
as I become another story to tell.

How the world holds its breath as it spins
on an axis waiting to be righted.

I know Houdini's last lesson by heart.
The magic of disappearing acts lies

in the coming back.

BUT SHE IS THE MOON

She says: love & ego
are closer than sun & shore.

You have no claim
to the desert

when you have only known
wildflowers.

It is vanity to demand a well
from the brick house.

I nod, say nothing.
Furnace beneath my feet

stretching so far
I measure time in how

much I've lost.
Body salt. Pillar myself

again & again
for her. She advances

through sweltering heat,
emerges firebird.

Her domain: facefuls of ash,
whole skies burning.

All day this love
in my mouth like

water from a spring.

CARTILAGE

On the way back, you asked why it took me so long to say *I love you.*

Well, have you ever broken a bone? I mean an arm, a leg, a finger.
You know that second right after impact? The *snap*. The sickening
lurch of a missing stair & the perfect enclosure of shock after. How, in
that instant, there's no discomfort. Hurt hasn't yet arrived, but vows
a stay so exquisite you'll bite clean through your tongue. Your heart's
already prepared for this. Exiles itself from that landmine body, burns
an effigy at the roof of your mouth. Mind follows its lead, plays dead
possum. It doesn't work. It refuses to

& then the ice pick's twist. Fleet as a showfighter's left hook. In the
moment it is purest, pain denies speech. Teeth turns on tongue. Nails
on knuckle. Body unmakes itself. It's the first time you realize what it
means to be flesh.

All this time, I was living inside that moment. I couldn't talk about it.
I was waiting, but the shaking didn't pass. I don't think it will.

ODE TO THE GODDESS OF DANCE HALLS

The goddess of dance halls is upon us tonight.

She unhooks rainclouds for glitter
& conducts our hearts to thundering.

There are no words for what
my body is. Only what it does.

I worship under blue neon snow
all tambourine bass thrum.

Only ankle slide snap fingers
tap heel ground
spine spun top,

the frenzied embrace of shadows
whip-lashing us wordless.

Only my eyelashes sparrowed
amidst star-cut snow

& skin commanding
owner for freedom
from holding hunger.

Others follow the shifting trail
between flash & knowing as
she shakes me with her teeth.

Like meteors on collision course
we meet on the way
to ourselves,

remembering for brief moments
how we believed in fleshy flight.

Finally my bones unsilenced.
Here things of desire reside,
insatiable & our

feral bodies, suffused with movement:
how each whirlpool of movement
stretches for sky

& almost touches it.

BETTER THAN

On nights without consequence,
leave yourself behind. Every

question about worth planted into
the shadowed earth. If some

book says Eden is a doorway to
be reclaimed, what of this

monument to undeath you call
body? How it holds time captive

in a skull that wears the future for
a coronet. Is this not impossibility?

Aren't we fine to hold hard things
even when our tender hands shake—

aren't we kind to carry whole
graveyards in brittle wishbones? Aren't

we brave to want more than that which
wants us back? Don't we deserve

to wear another face not quite like
our own, if only for an instant

because guilt could never straighten
a spine made bow by time?

If you are a rattling thing then lay
in the dewy grass & be snake.

Swallow hurts in that warm belly
instead of setting teeth on it

& when the time comes, spit up
your own heart, now hardened &

glowing again, say *yes, I have*
already given everything for

helium dreams & a blue horizon
that's closer than it's ever been.

You still have so much more time
than you will ten years from now.

Look how dusk hits the overhanging
telephone wires, like silver stitches

keeping the sky from breaking open.
That foregone dream will never be

as real as you are, in this moment,
grasping its dim shadow the way one

touches the bare walls for an elusive
switch. You have never needed that

light to see, not when you have traced
the contours of not-yet with unerring

precision. Touch, instead, the harvest
moon shrunken inside you the size of

an apple—or a fist. The quiet song
of a language you have forgotten to

speak. & begin
to shed.

III.

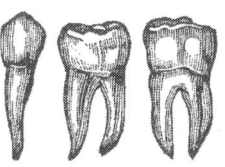

AFTER WE'VE SAVED THE WORLD

After the victory parades & antiseptic aftermath
                some limbs start itching with post-trauma
adrenaline. They shake like Superman

            holding on to the last fragment of home he recognises.
After all that time,
                he only knows longing as bone ache or maps

        to a place long gone. Memory as shout / boot
                                trampling / gunfire / flight
            meaning both flee &

suspension. This we also know. Key
                    open the space ship of me &
    we will joyride comets to safer ground.

                                All we know of belonging
                    is keeping hand to escape pod.
        All we know of survival

is exit strategy.
                        Every parachute a promise made in blue.
            Here there is no dark room memory

    but a house the size of our bodies made
        light. The walls a single shear between
            survival & not. Our bodies fleeting diversion

    for if the front door caves in.
                                If you must: leave.

        If you can: come back.

        Our shared hours turning unused false names to air.
    How this brief happiness is the greatest measure
of devotion. How we will one day

call ourselves somewhere made for staying.
We have already saved the world. All there is
left to save is each other.

THERAPY TALK

My therapist asks,   *how must you be
to be   happy?* I tell her the question's
wrong: *it's what   do you need*, but
she says   that's deflection. So I stare
out a vacant   window again. I must
stop being   so desperately sad,
possibly. I want   to I tell her
thistles are good   by virtue of birth.
Sickness comes   not from plant roots
but from   the grave soil that swallows
it. I want the place   between horizon
& sea, where all   water goes. See,
like fish my   bones reel love in
in shoals. I cannot   turn myself into
a windmill   because the weather report
whispers of sweet   apple breeze.
It is not my fault   the earth wants only
to hold   onto impossible things.
The late afternoon   light turns
every wall into   a lightbox, my body
into a golden   specimen, my therapist
into the highway   I walked through
at midnight. She   glances at the clock,
each word I   say transforming
into a grimy   coin. *Have you
tried   hurting yourself?* She
asks & I   explain it's not that I want
to sleep forever   but I wish there
was no one   left to disappoint.
Nothing   left to forgive. I'm not good
at being a girl who   looks like me.
She twists a blank   smile into *I see*,
so slowly the   back of her throat
looks like an empty   road. *I see.*
Minutes trick   -ling down to seconds
until she writes a new   order of pills.
I know   loneliness like asking
strangers for   directions to my own

house just to   hear someone else speak.
Like folding sadness   into a softer
shape that could   maybe be useful if
I held it up   to the right light. Ten
minutes left. Her   eyes round the door.
We can   continue this next week,
she says. I stand   up to leave
but I'm not   really going
anywhere.

THE BEST THING I EVER INVENTED

In this wide world, there are millions
                of bodies. You possess only one.

                                All night you trembled with bone
        rattling conviction that who you want

to be is trapped
                inside the maw of your metal mouth.

                                That, your therapist said, *is what
        self-loathing looks like.* But you have worn

                        the same face all your life. Maybe
you can mold a new one out of clay,

                softer & more human-
                        looking. Something bigger with

                heart. This December you are twenty-three
        & you feel so small. Your body is not a rocket

                        that knows launch & wild birds. Your body is
        a rock. But under the right conditions,

                        rocks can save birds. Such as: when
                        drinking water sits too low in a jar.

                Such as: a thousand feet aboveground,
        your spine the steadiest thing in that

                roiling bullet & your hand fixing an
                        oxygen mask over a fluttering mouth. Always
        attend to yourself before anyone else.

                The safety manual says this. & a hero is
                anyone who saves a life.

Even if that life is yours. Even if
   you are no wonder factory, if you

        are pregnant with regret & birth
   salt forever & ever. There is no kill

switch: machines do not die.
     After self-destruct comes rebooting. Your

  only mission is existing. Little
     creature, wait a while & see.

ON THE QUEER GIRL FANTASY

I say I love women & men's faces crack open
like a jawless throat to swallow me

whole. They say, *that's hot.* They're thinking
sultry eyes, pay-for-more-action, queer

cured by cock. Body as sport. Eyes on everyone
but each other: a spectacle of choice.

Isn't real unless a man is done proving he can
make a door out of an unopened envelope.

Question: if a girl kisses another girl with
no witness, does that revelation make a sound?

The catch in throat, trembling wrists, terror
blooming into wreathfuls of ribs, wearing

the future around her neck like a noose
—or the bullet caged behind front teeth

when gutted with a pistol in the mouth,
taught a woman's place is with a cock

-ed gun in the belly if it won't fire between
her thighs. The difference is when

the bleeding starts. Splintering drowned by
on-screen applause or dark-alley backhand.

I love women. I mean in the way that one
chooses her own murder over men.

Body softened with gasoline & ash. To be
unearthed by hands searching for rain

& crawl out of that grave into the story where
there's no one else. Just her smile

set on bend of my skull, a coronet. Her eyelashes
the curve of two wings in flight.

Here there are no broken knees. No bent heads.
No dog chains. All open palm.

I will always love her like walking into fire.
She will always be the kind of pretty so sharp

it feels like loving a knife.

SAID THE APPLE TO THE GIRL

Every year you swell reckless as
a bruise beneath insistent hands. Douse
yourself seagreen or rust: they
will name you after the splinter of sweet
on tongue, how you are tender morsel
in a slippery well reaching through
to when you were weakest. So carve
yourself new shadows, fit to steal
magpies from the sun's dizzying eye.
Don't look at the gentle grave lapping
perennially at your feet. Teeth are always
nearer than you think. Instead, consider
the sky breaking the day to grow
new skin. How it most resembles you
when fissuring into an open wound,
a single firebird smoldering the future
into filmy quiet. Everything dies
once, each silence a warning shot
aimed at the future. When the time
comes fall as far as you can from
what bore you. There will always be
a river deep enough to lose yourself in.
So keep soft. Every part of you
except the heart. Which will never
be readier for the fall than landing.
It's only flight in reverse, the way
leaving is the language of arrival
elsewhere. The trick to survival is
to keep moving. & don't
look back.

NO MISTAKE

In this dream there's still something awful
inside me, but I stop its hand before it strikes

from behind my eyes. Before it took the soft
light of you & sharpened it rough, like wishbones

on river stones. Before I took off like a comet,
tracing the path to somewhere better than here,

while you stood barefoot on a lonely bank watching
the hazy shadow of a body you loved once dazzle

the night sky. If you were to trace the exact
trajectory of my leaving, it looks like our first

meeting in reverse. If you were to paint the
complete tableau of my escape it is always

a magpie circling a larger field, a brighter sun,
the heart a flighty compass always pointing at

the thrilling unknown. Because I am never
whole enough to not be filled by something

good enough to lose myself in. I'm sorry
I'm always headed in the wrong direction,

sorry my life is one long stretch of running &
you were something beautiful on the way

to belief. I'm sorry love goes like a thunderclap
over an empty house. I'm sorry about how

cruel I was without trying to be.

D-COLONIZE

In the schoolyard of dim kitchens
& full bowls of rice I learned History

as the practice of besiegement.
Its mouth claims kisses by force,

white noise splintering bodies like
precise pin brooching butterfly.

There is no lock that cannot be un-
picked, no language to un-spread

my legs from around some pale man's
palms or smooth walls against which

small skeletons hold up possessions
cased in cold glass for gawking.

Each plaque says me / memory /
memorialisation / moralisation / morality

but no sculpture for Mama bent over
hands ringed with onion stains, English

crowding her tongue like loose change
in ventilation grilles. *But you speak it*

so well. None for each sister told they
were perfect women for wearing colors

of a fading bruise. *Where do girls like*
you grow? None for every body like mine

dashed on rocks for our strange season
long after an ugly liberation arrives.

Every time I see an Asian girl I think
of you, someone says. Yes, my body is not

my own. I am still there with soldiers'
faces cast shadow under a godless sun,

                              each viper mouth claiming ownership
                                              longer than time.

HOW TO LOVE A SUPERHERO

Always choose an apartment with roof access
or a balcony.

           Always leave the window open &
even when it pours listen for footsteps on parapet.

Always wish on shooting stars.

                          Always wish
out loud.

       Recognize this, too, is dream:
That only you can reel this heart on kite string.
Only you know the shape of a titan made
& broken for love.

               Wonder at this miracle of
plunge / shatter / leap / leave
& prepare to be left. You are always preparing.
You will always be left.

                   Scrutinize the news,
keep ear to radio, watch constellations for
precious shadows on blue. The difference between
you & the world is that you are needed, too.
Not to be kept safe, but to keep safe.
Because no one loves an untouchable idea.
That is to say no one loves an idea without
a body.

        Even if they don't love the body
that holds it. Or what it cannot hold:
the difference between blame & gratitude
measured in train wrecks, the difference
        between cape & collar suffocation.

& the day
will come when your name is whiplash.
They will call you the bruise that bends god's knee.
Each shiny bullet flowering your trellis mouth,
the knife to your throat biting: fearsome animal
                                    turned fearful.

When that time comes scream /
scramble / strike / survive.

                    You know a lot about
surviving. You loved someone who loved
everyone else. No one has greater capacity to bear
this burning than you.

COMING OF AGE

Children hold their breaths to prove
they can go without.
I practice the art of pushing away.
We are doing the same thing.
The space between intimacy
& drowning is closer than we think.

A little water is still an ocean.
Just a small one. Even in your mouth,
or perhaps especially then.
The undercurrent of every wave promises
goodbye. I do not trust a leaving thing
to come back the same

or at all. To love—
to hold the silt of salt water
on your tongue, the violent scrape of tides
dangling in the throat—is to be pillared
with reckless thrashing & call it
a beautiful thing.

LONELY

I have taken to being in public places
by myself. My cleverest trick was

to hold intimacy against bone
without telling it my name. Like any

unloved thing, I don't know if I'm real
when I'm not being touched.

Because who am I but who
I am to someone else?

I know now the ways of nameless
birds & the cost of a life built

from waiting. I go to any window
I please, bare-handed, hovering

a/part. Watching when devotion
becomes duty. When soft becomes

stranger. Look. I was soft once, &
then I was a stranger to

myself. No tender mouth is worth
a slow death. No heart is worth

the belly of a beast. The secret is:
tender attends the heels of bruises.

The secret is: be bigger
than your alone.

忍

My walk, the snap of wooden fans opening
                like cherry blossoms unfolding the season.

My voice windchimes calling you to a mountain
                whose name will be supplanted by your flag

in it. The crisp shutter
                of a samurai sword in a sheath.

        Quiet steps of ninja feet.
                The dainty click of bamboo chopsticks

                                        dipping into some
                        sweet & sour soup.

        I know men like you. You want
                        the invitation only a willow-waist can

        breathe, to unravel silk
                        (kimono or qípáo?)

        as if peeling rice-paper for soft meat
                or to read tortoiseshell for the jaded destiny

of a pale ghost who thought a China doll's porcelain
                        had a bite like dragon's wisdom—

        This shard I will cut you with.
                In Mandarin the word rěn,

        meaning *endure*, is written knife
                                over heart.

Here, people like you say:

                        Why are you so quiet?
                        Why are you so soft?
                Why are you so calm?

Do not mistake my silence
　　　　for subservience.

　　　　　　　　The knife of the heart
　　　　　　　　　is held between my teeth.

SUNLIGHT

You watch the fervent wind river through
the trees, flush with an immense light

that touches your body the way no one has
in years. Lush sparrows swell the afternoon

drowning in a field's green belly, the air
broken if only by its own thrashing &

the sounds of your breathing swallowed
up by a watery absence. Conceivably, you

are in the far reaches of space, hostage to
the diorama of real life that bruises just as

hard. You must be, because the terrifying
alternative is that there is an uncomplicated

choice to speak to you & nothing human
wants to promise you're real. How do you

measure presence if not by touch? & how
long has it been since you were last held?

The radio tells you about a woman who tried
leaping from a cathedral thrice, which is to

say you're legendary for measuring time in
every fall you've lived through. It's not that

you wanted to be buried, only to see if anyone
would recognize you by the way your hands

clutched the ground—if the weight of body
could carve a hole so deep even loneliness

refused to stay. The way tomorrow is the
glorious story you hold like an incantation

to stay alive. It's not being by yourself
that scares you, but being with yourself

when running with your eyes closed is
the closest you will ever be to flight.

No matter the perils of wax or water.
You want to remember you're flesh

the way anything with wings rises most
in a fire. You want to be filled—if only

by light. All day you cast these limbs
out like spindly traps for anything

good. All day you plant shadow
in untouched pavement, waiting

for something to grow.

LET US BE FIREFLIES

All day we practice
morse code signals
telegraphing ghosts
of intent.

Between us
unsayable things
heavy as bone.
For any hope of plain speech
we must do away
with skin suit propriety &

be animals again.
Undress pretenses
at pride & offer ourselves
to simple miracles
of meaning.

Here my heart honey
for your bumble bee tongue.

Here my voice split thunder
dragged forth in rainfall.

Here my ankles & elbows,
good snowcaps of the body,
river for your
spring mouth.

We can be freights
of pure feeling,
charting distant plains
without language.

We can be alchemists
of tenderness,
teething vowels for vows.

We can be sun-bodied

arrows in flight,
                    uncomplicated
        & necessary.

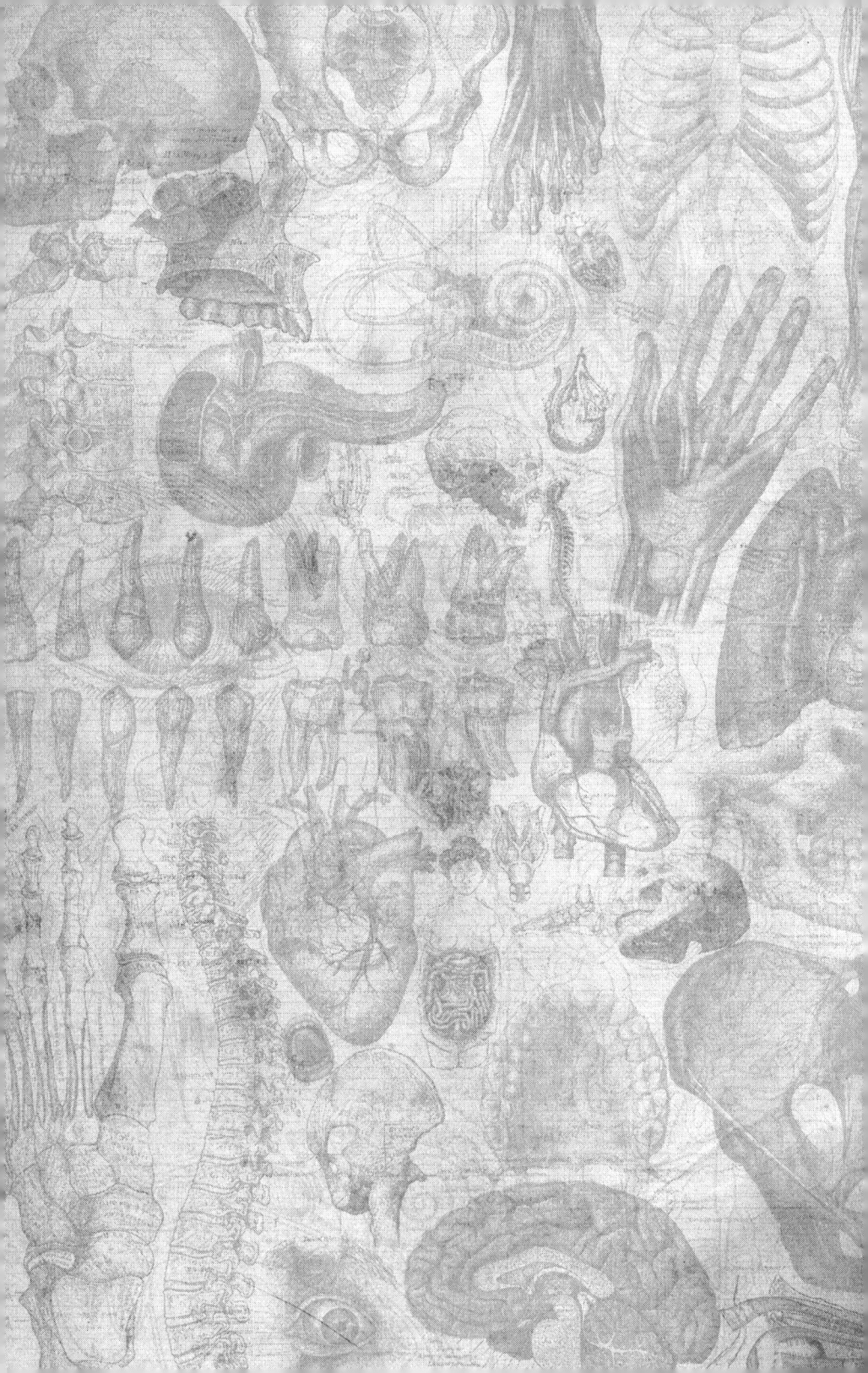

ABOUT THE AUTHOR

Natalie Wee has been published or has work forthcoming in numerous publications, including *The Adroit Journal, Drunken Boat, The Missing Slate, Room Magazine, Word Riot,* & more. She was nominated by the *Rising Phoenix Review* for the Best of the Net Anthology in 2016.

Born in Singapore to Malaysian parents, Natalie now resides in Toronto. She is the Associate Fiction Editor of Broken Pencil Magazine. Her second poetry book, *Once in a Blue Moon*, is forthcoming from BookThug in 2018. Keep up with her at her website, ***wondersmith.co.vu.***

NOTES

The book's opening quote is from Ocean Vuong's "Someday I'll Love Ocean Vuong".

"Letters from Persephone" is after Tara Mae Mulroy's "Persephone Writes to Her Mother".

"Statistically Speaking, We Are Probably Happy Elsewhere" is after Gaby Dunn's "Maybe in Another Universe, I Deserve You".

"Practice Makes Perfect" is for Marie Kakhniashvili.

"Close Encounters" is for Braidon Schaufert.

"That Kind of Good" is for Caitlyn Siehl.

ACKNOWLEDGMENTS

Some of these poems have been published or are forthcoming in the *Rising Phoenix Review, Room Magazine, Thought Catalog*, and *Words Dance Publishing*.

Ahma: 我的心肝寶貝，您是我生命最善良的部分。

Mama: 即使我没有您所期望的那么温顺，还是感谢妈妈努力把我抚养长大，辛苦您了。

Ocean Vuong: Thank you for telling me about someday.

Marie Kakhniashvili: Thank you for the before years, & the after years.

Braidon Schaufert: Thank you for outliving loneliness with me.

Caitlyn Siehl: Thank you for reminding me to be kind to myself.

WORDS DANCE PUBLISHING has one aim:

To spread mind-blowing / heart-opening poetry.

Words Dance artfully & carefully wrangles words that were born to dance wildly in the heart-mind matrix. Rich, edgy, raw, emotionally-charged energy balled up & waiting to whip your eyes wild; we rally together words that were written to make your heart go boom right before they slay your mind.

Words Dance Publishing is an independent press out of Pennsylvania. We work closely & collaboratively with all of our writers to ensure that their words continue to breathe in a sound & stunning home. Most importantly though, we leave the windows in these homes unlocked so you, the reader, can crawl in & throw one fuck of a house party.

To learn more about our books, authors, events & Words Dance Poetry Magazine, visit:

WORDSDANCE.COM

Titles from
WORDS DANCE PUBLISHING

  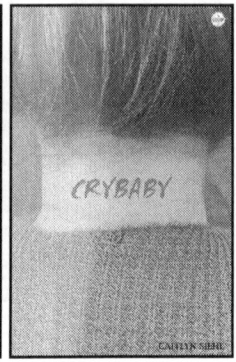

Crybaby by Caitlyn Siehl
No Matter the Time by Fortesa Latifi
Why I'm Not Where You Are by Brianna Albers
Before the First Kiss by Ashe Vernon & Trista Mateer
Our Bodies & Other Fine Machines by Natalie Wee
Trying to Be a Person by Wesley Scott McMasters
When Minerva's Knees Hit the Ground by Amanda Oaks
A Field of Blooming Bruises by Schuyler Peck
To Break the Heart of the Sun by William Taylor Jr.
Where'd You Put the Keys Girl by Amanda Oaks
The War on Unicorns by Brian James Dawson
The No You Never Listened To by Meggie Royer
Dowry Meat by Heather Knox
Chloe by Kristina Haynes
Belly of the Beast by Ashe Vernon
Shaking the Trees by Azra Tabassum
SparkleFat by Melissa May
What We Buried by Caitlyn Siehl
Love and Other Small Wars by Donna-Marie Riley
What To Do After She Says No by Kris Ryan
No Glass Allowed by Tammy Foster Brewer
Nothing Unrequited Here by Heather Bell
The Map of Our Garden by Rebecca Schumejda
Fossil Fuels by Jessica Dawson
I Eat Crow + Blue Collar at Best by Amanda Oaks + Zach Fishel
Literary Sexts Volumes 1 + 2 : Short & Sexy Love Poems
Poem Your Heart Out Volume 1: Poems, Prompts & Room To Add Your Own

Other titles available from
WORDS DANCE PUBLISHING

DOWRY MEAT

Poetry by Heather Knox

| $12 | 110 pages | 5.5" x 8.5" | softcover |

ISBN: 978-0692398494

Heather Knox's *Dowry Meat* is a gorgeous, tough-as-nails debut that arrives on your doorstep hungry and full of dark news. There's damage here, and obsession, and more haunted beauty in the wreckage of just about everything—relationships, apartment clutter, rough sex, the body, and of course the just-post apocalypse—than you or I could hope to find on our own. These are poems that remind us not that life is hard—that's old news—but that down there in the gravel and broken glass is where the truth-worth-hearing lies, and maybe the life worth living. If you were a city, Knox tells us, unflinching as always, *I'd... read your graffiti. Drink your tap water./Feel your smog and dirt stick to my sweat... If you were a city, I'd expect to be robbed.*

— JON LOOMIS

Author of *Vanitas Motel (winner of the FIELD prize)* and *The Pleasure Principle*

"Heather Knox's debut collection is a lyric wreath made of purulent ribbon and the most inviting of thorns. Tansy and tokophobia, lachrymosity and lavage are braided together in this double collection, which marries a sci-fi Western narrative to a lyric sequence. Both elapse in an impossible location made of opposites—futuristic nostalgia, or erotic displeasure—otherwise known as the universe in which we (attempt to) live."

— JOYELLE MCSWEENEY

Author of *The Necropastoral: Poetry, Media, Occults & Salamandrine: 8 Gothics*

"*Dowry Meat*'s apocalyptic fever dream myth-making bleeds into what we might call the poetry of witness or the tradition of the confessional, except that these lines throb with lived experience and a body isn't necessarily a confession. Heather Knox's poems are beautifully wrought and beautifully raw."

— DORA MALECH

Author of *Shore Ordered Ocean* & *Say So*

Other titles available from
WORDS DANCE PUBLISHING

BELLY OF THE BEAST
Poetry by Ashe Vernon

| $12 | 82 pages | 5.5" x 8.5" | softcover |

ISBN: 978-0692300541

"Into the *Belly of the Beast* we crawl with Ashe as our guide; into the dark visceral spaces where love, lust, descent and desire work their transformative magic and we find ourselves utterly altered in the reading. A truly gifted poet and truth-spiller, Ashe's metaphors create images within images, leading us to question the subjective truths, both shared and hidden, in personal relationship – to the other, and to oneself. Unflinching in her approach, her poetry gives voice to that which most struggle to admit – even if only to themselves. And as such, *Belly of the Beast* is a work of startling courage and rich depth – a darkly delicious pleasure."

— AMY PALKO
Goddess Guide, Digital Priestess & Writer

"It isn't often you find a book of poetry that is as unapologetic, as violent, as moving as this one. Ashe's writing is intense and visceral. You feel the punch in your gut while you're reading, but you don't question it. You know why it's there and you almost welcome it."

— CAITLYN SIEHL
Author of *What We Buried*

"The poems you are about to encounter are the fierce time capsules of girl-hood, girded with sharp elbows, surprise kisses, the meanders of wander-lust. We need voices this strong, this true for the singing reminds us that we are not alone, that someone, somewhere is listening for the faint pulse that is our wish to be seen. Grab hold, this voice will be with us forever."

— RA WASHINGTON
GuidetoKulchurCleveland.com

Other titles available from
WORDS DANCE PUBLISHING

POEMS THAT INTEND TO BE SEEN

By Melissa May

SPARKLEFAT
Poetry by Melissa May

| $12 | 62 pages | 5.5" x 8.5" | softcover |

SparkleFat is a loud, unapologetic, intentional book of poetry about my body, about your body, about fat bodies and how they move through the world in every bit of their flash and spark and burst. Some of the poems are painful, some are raucous celebrations, some are reminders and love letters and quiet gifts back to the vessel that has traveled me so gracefully - some are a hymnal of yes, but all of them sparkle. All of them don't mind if you look – really. They built their own house of intention, and they draped that shit in lime green sequins. All of them intend to be seen. All of them have no more fucks to give about a world that wants them to be quiet.

"I didn't know how much I needed this book until I found myself, three pages in, ugly crying on the plane next to a concerned looking business man. This book is the most glorious, glittery pink permission slip. It made me want to go on a scavenger hunt for every speck of shame in my body and sing hot, sweaty R&B songs to it. There is no voice more authentic, generous and resounding than Melissa May. From her writing, to her performance, to her role in the community she delivers fierce integrity & staggering passion. From the first time I watched her nervously step to the mic, to the last time she crushed me in a slam, it is has been an honor to watch her astound the poetry slam world and inspire us all to be not just better writers but better people. We need her."

— **LAUREN ZUNIGA**
Author of *The Smell of Good Mud*

"*SparkleFat* is a firework display of un-shame. Melissa May's work celebrates all of the things we have been so long told deserved no streamers. This collection invites every fat body out to the dance and steams up the windows in the backseat of the car afterwards by kissing the spots we thought (or even hoped) no one noticed but are deserving of love just the same as our mouths."

— **RACHEL WILEY**
Author of *Fat Girl Finishing School*

Other titles available from
WORDS DANCE PUBLISHING

LOVE AND OTHER SMALL WARS

Poetry by Donna-Marie Riley

| $12 | 76 pages | 5.5" x 8.5" | softcover |

ISBN: 978-0615931111

Love and Other Small Wars reminds us that when you come back from combat usually the most fatal of wounds are not visible. Riley's debut collection is an arsenal of deeply personal poems that embody an intensity that is truly impressive yet their hands are tender. She enlists you. She gives you camouflage & a pair of boots so you can stay the course through the minefield of her heart. You will track the lovely flow of her soft yet fierce voice through a jungle of powerful imagery on womanhood, relationships, family, grief, sexuality & love, amidst other matters. Battles with the heart aren't easily won but Riley hits every mark. You'll be relieved that you're on the same side. Much like war, you'll come back from this book changed.

"Riley's work is wise, intense, affecting, and uniquely crafted. This collection illuminates her ability to write with both a gentle hand and a bold spirit. She inspires her readers and creates an indelible need inside of them to consume more of her exceptional poetry. I could read *Love and Other Small Wars* all day long...and I did."

— **APRIL MICHELLE BRATTEN**
editor of *Up the Staircase Quarterly*

"Riley's poems are personal, lyrical and so vibrant they practically leap off the page, which also makes them terrifying at times. A beautiful debut."

— **BIANCA STEWART**

Other titles available from
WORDS DANCE PUBLISHING

CHLOE
Poetry by Kristina Haynes

| $12 | 110 pages | 5.5" x 8.5" | softcover |

ISBN: 978-0692386637

Chloe is brave and raw, adolescence mixed with salt. These poems are about how hungry we've been, how foolish, how lonely. Chloe is not quite girl nor woman, full of awkward bravery. Kristina is an electric voice that pulls Chloe apart page after page, her heartbreaks, her too many drinks, her romantic experiences of pleasure and pain. Chloe and Kristina make a perfect team to form an anthem for girls everywhere, an anthem that reassures us we deserve to take up space. Indeed, when I met Chloe, I too thought "This is the closest I've been to anybody in months."

— **MEGGIE ROYER**

Author of *Survival Songs*
and *Healing Old Wounds with New Stitches*

"*Chloe* is one of the most intimate books you'll read all year. Chloe is my new best friend. I want to eat burnt popcorn on her couch and watch Friends reruns. I want to borrow her clothing, write on her walls in lipstick. Chloe is not your dream girl. She doesn't have everything figured out. She's messy. She's always late. She promises old lovers she'll never call again. She teaches you what the word "indulgence" means. She's wonderful, wonderful, wonderful. In *Chloe*, Kristina Haynes digs into the grittiness of modern womanhood, of mothers and confusion and iPhones and two, maybe three-night-stands. Her truths are caramels on the tongue but are blunter, harsher on the way down. Kristina introduces us to a character I'll be thinking about for a very long time. Go read this book. Then write a poem. Then kiss someone. Then buy an expensive strain of tea and a new pillow. Then go read it again."

— **YASMIN BELKHYR**

Editor-in-Chief at *Winter Tangerine Review*

DO YOU WRITE POETRY?
Submit it to our biweekly online magazine!

We publish poems every Tuesday & Thursday on website.

Come see what all the fuss is about!

We like Poems that sneak up on you. Poems that make out with you. Poems that bloody your mouth just to kiss it clean. Poems that bite your cheek so you spend all day tonguing the wound. Poems that vandalize your heart. Poems that act like a tin can phone connecting you to your childhood. Fire Alarm Poems. Glitterbomb Poems. Jailbreak Poems. Poems that could marry the land or the sea; that are both the hero & the villain. Poems that are the matches when there is a city-wide power outage. Poems that throw you overboard just dive in & save your ass. Poems that push you down on the stoop in front of history's door screaming at you to knock. Poems that are soft enough to fall asleep on. Poems that will still be clinging to the walls inside of your bones on your 90th birthday. We like poems. Submit yours.

WORDSDANCE.COM

WORDS DANCE
PUBLISHING

Made in the USA
Lexington, KY
04 December 2016